I0224199

Wonder-filled and Strange

poems by

Elizabeth A. Gibson

Finishing Line Press
Georgetown, Kentucky

Wonder-filled and Strange

In gratitude:
Mother, Father, Brother
and for Julie Fawcett,
friend and superhero

Copyright © 2025 by Elizabeth A. Gibson
ISBN 979-8-89990-216-1 First Edition
All rights reserved under International and Pan-American Copyright Conventions.
No part of this book may be reproduced in any manner whatsoever without written
permission from the publisher, except in the case of brief quotations embodied in
critical articles and reviews.

ACKNOWLEDGMENTS

"Not Shaped Like a Fist," published in *Cutthroat: A Journal of the Arts*
"The Vigil," published under a different title ("The Holding") in *Two Hawks
Quarterly*
"Coming Apart in Puerto Vallarta," *The Tishman Review*
"Solitude and Spaciousness in Hopper," *Iconoclast Magazine*
"Hunter," *Autumn Leaves,* a Barnes & Noble Anthology

Publisher: Leah Huete de Maines
Editor: Christen Kincaid
Cover Art: Julie Fawcett
Author Photo: Nancy McCrohan
Cover Design: Elizabeth Maines McCleavy

Order online: www.finishinglinepress.com
also available on amazon.com

Author inquiries and mail orders:
Finishing Line Press
PO Box 1626
Georgetown, Kentucky 40324
USA

Contents

The Vigil

The vigil is over; Martina is gone.
Her children have returned to their homes
which seem now so strange—

the red and yellow marigolds
that once brightened the yard look diminished,
and a grey film lingers over the sofas and chairs.

It is as if the struggle between moments and worlds
that held Martina for days—

the ancient drumbeat of "More life! More life!"
that made her fight without knowing she fought
and dream without knowing she dreamt;

that shaped the rhythm of her final days,
holding them all entranced and exhausted
until her last breath had passed—

it is as if that world were the real world,
the normal one; the one they didn't know existed
until it held them, too.

Solitude and Spaciousness in Hopper

A quiet inwardness pervades:

A man bends over a rake, combing
up the leaves; a woman sits on a bed,
leaning toward an open window.

In each painting, the sun's
stream is white, it's angle wide.

The mood is receptive, the mind
diffuse and expansive, like the light;

like an empty room in Hopper,
appealing and spare.

Light falling on shared places
(lamp-light, sunlight, the moon's
glow) accentuates the space
between individuals, a privacy

in which separateness
need not mean loneliness,

but might instead mean solitude,
mean peace.

Seek There Wonder

Where "thee" is wonder, seek there beauty,
seek there grace:

in the raccoon's mask and the monkey's reach;
in the garlicky scent of a skunk's spray,
and in the bite of each.

Seek thee in the bloom and wave of the sea anemone,
and in the muscular suck of an outgoing tide;
in the shark's teeth and a seagull's glide.

Seek thee in thunder's growl and a black bird's wing;
in the complex coil of instructions tucked into the folds
of every living thing.

Seek thee, seek thee!

In the heart's lift at the lean of light;
in the squirrel's leap and a child's delight;

in the farthest stretch of the ocean's deep;
and in the long, soft arc of a willow's sweep.

The Visit

When death came,
she was lying on her side in a hospital bed,
ninety-five pounds of fragility and iron,
nose and forehead pressed against the railing,
her body quaking with the effort of every breath.

Death came,
lifted off the oxygen mask,
placed one hand beneath her shoulder
and another under her hip,
prepared to take her with him.

Her concentration broken—
the concentration of the dying
on the labor of holding onto life—
she opened an exhausted brown eye and said,
"I want a root-beer float."

This gave death a bit of a pause,
not because she didn't want to go
—after all, few do—
but because she so clearly had
other things on her mind.

He tried again.

"Rose," he whispered into her ear, "Rose."
Roused, she rolled painfully onto her back,
fixed him with an aggrieved brown glare,
and repeated, "I want a root-beer float!"

Death was offended—so serious a matter,
so unappreciatively brushed aside!—
and ever-so-slightly intimidated.

He returned her to the bed,
gave his cape a frustrated twirl
and muttered as he retreated,
"I'll be back."

And he was.

Coming Apart in Puerto Vallarta

The sea at body temperature (too warm), and brown, too,
like river wash from a mountain in the spring. Not

travel-market blue or *azure*, but the mud-brown
of poverty, of the village itself after a storm

pushed through it last year.
Waiters and bar owners cajole us from doorways—

langosta, vino, bueno! They smile, beckon, laugh,
tease, their brown eyes wary with contempt—

for our naïveté, our emptiness; for having so much
and not knowing what we have.

We lounged away the afternoons in beach chairs,
drinking G&T's and diving into the tepid waves.

Women in long skirts weaved between the chairs selling necklaces
while bare-chested men hawked jet skis at the water's edge;

we rarely lifted our sunglasses to meet their eyes.
No breeze at night, not even a star in the sky—

the air hung too heavy for that; buoyant
like salt water, only the clouds could float.

At 4 a.m. we sat on the beach, nursing gin.
An iguana happened by, grinning. "Hey, Amigos!"

he said, "You want to buy a hat?"
Might have been the booze talking, a figment

of our weary ennui, mentally slumming as we were,
as distant from the damped-down longing in our hearts

as we were from each other; as distant as the moon was
from the sand between our toes.

People Swimming and Wading have Drowned Here

The jogger tore off her shirt and walked into the surf,
a grey mid-March wash of foam,
the water waist-high near the shore.

She waded in slowly, as though the water were 70 degrees
rather than 50, and hopped up
to let her belly take a wave.

Over near the seawall sat a pile of belongings,
someone's faded black jeans, a tangle of
shirts and socks, a chewed-up plastic bowl.

Their owner hitched her hips down the boardwalk stairs,
a square-shaped woman once black now
the sun-burnt, thrice-baked brown

of those who live permanently outdoors.
"The waves are shit today," a thin, stubble-face man said,
hovering near the woman's circle of stuff.

Leaning over the seawall to address her directly he continued,
"No action at all." The woman ignored him
and sat down on the sand, looking out at the water

mouthing a piece of hard candy, her lips disappeared to the task.
Down by the ocean's edge, the jogger returned to shore
pulled on her shirt and crouched to her ankles,

hugging her breasts to her thighs.
The fog ate up the remains of the sun
as we all gazed out to sea—

the homeless woman, the wave-minded man,
the cool, wet jogger and me—
held in the same eternal moment,

breathing the sea's breath,
feeling the tick-tock of the tide
beating against our lungs.

Meditation in a Cathedral

"The Word was made Flesh in order to make me God."
—*Saint Teresa of Avila*

I.

The rose petals drew me in, velvety and bright,
spilling across the floor and flowing out the open doors.
I followed them up the steps and sat down in the last row of pews,
mahogany benches worn smooth from years of use.

It'd been a long time since I'd been inside a Christian church.
Stately it was, ceilings high in the Cathedral style, windows tall,
hand-crafted panes telling the story of humanity's rise and fall.

A cross of stained oak, dressed in palm leaves, hung above the altar,
the body of Christ stretched across it, a frail figure carved in pale
    wood,
his face soft with the sorrow of understanding
what some were willing to sacrifice for a dream of eternal life.

From elsewhere in the church, an organ offered up its signature
    sound—
the long note of mourning used for celebration and funeral alike—
and the regular Sunday procession began:

Altar boys carried the instruments of mass up the center aisle
followed by deacon and priest, walking with meditative deliberation,
rosary beads dangling from their fingers.

After the greetings, the readings began:
the deacon delivered Exodus 20 in a practiced voice,
then used Mark to explain that, once given,

the Word must be nourished by the listener into action,
must be rightly sown in order to bear fruit, not stones.

After each reading, voices rose in ritual response,
and the 'specially penitent struck her breast three times:
I have sinned through my own fault, in what I have done,
and what I have failed to do
seeking, by this action, forgiveness, its grace and relief.

The choir sang as the congregants queued patiently for
    Communion,
and I watched as one by one, they tilted their heads
and accepted the Host on their tongue: swallowing the seed,
internalizing the Word.

As I watched, I thought of St. Teresa's passion,
of her hunger for knowledge and goodness,
and I considered what her words might mean—
that Christ embodied the Word's intent, and that
to absorb the communion wafer is to become,
like a god, both immortal and wise.

Yet when I think of the Word, and of words,
I think not of a god's proscriptions,
but of the special ability language gives us
to clarify and complicate our perceptions,
to obscure and illuminate our intentions—
to shape the world by creating and assigning a word.

The image of the dying Christ on the cross disturbed me as a child,
and perplexed me as a young adult for it seemed to me then,
as it does to me now, that the work of salvation belongs to each
    private self,
and to the private self only—that the path to wisdom is dotted not
with the footsteps of Christ carrying us, but
with the imprint of our own feet bearing the weight of us,
of our circumstances and the choices that we make.

II.

After Communion, the parishioners knelt in silent prayer
as the priest cleaned the chalice and plate and put them away.
The service I'd stumbled into that Sunday morning
was much like the weekend masses of my youth,
including the closing ritual, a favorite when young:

Standing to shake hands with our near neighbors in the pew,
we exchanged this blessing:
"May peace be with you," the woman in front of me said,
"And also with you," said I as I took her hand.

The priest wished us Godspeed and we left the church soon after,
stepping past the sad-eyed statue of Mary and over the drying rose
   petals,
still elegant though browning at the edges,
the hope of that blessing carried with us,
a bit of wisdom, human-made.

Wonder-filled and Strange

In the beginning was desire,
was water, was dark.

A charge sparked the emptiness
and space expanded from the smallest point,
time freed in the stirring,
finally able to move.

Hydrogen and helium combined in the heat,
speckling the universe with a million suns and stars.

Or was it the breath of god that created the galaxies
and showered them with planets?

Which god? Yahweh, or Brahma?
A single god, was it, or many—
a pantheon of Titians, or
a council of spirit chiefs?

And was intention behind the creation
or happenstance only?

Perhaps there are many worlds,
or maybe only this one—
lavish and unpredictable,
wonder-filled and strange.

Beryl McGregor

The first time I saw her, I thought:

> *She ought to be riding horses*
> *across a long, low prairie*
> *where the horizon is so far distant*
> *you need a wide mind just to see it.*

Instead, she was leaning on a balustrade
      looking over the spillway,
wrists hanging over the rail,
      one black-leathered boot resting on the bottom rung.

Below her, ancient pumps, hidden
      behind heavy, pulsing curtains of water,
pushed five tons of filthy, writhing river
      over the dam's rough edge.

The power of the water's fall
      sent waves of wind through the air,
and blew Beryl's hair, now damp,
      behind her shoulders into the sky.

She lit a cigarette and exhaled into the mist.
      Her face was a wary plain and in her eyes
was the difference between a city under rain
      and rain falling on the open range.

She flicked the cigarette into the foam
      and watched it churn on a wave,
bubbling against the dam's crude wall—

water flowing over,
      water building up.

The Picture

The painted canvas yielded to grass
as I stepped over the frame and walked inside.

There was a pond and a boy
and in the distance there were mountains,
big ones with broad bases
that made the landscape blue from side to side.

The air was warm and still and evening
was a pale orange glow moving up the trees.
I found a path and took it to the boy,
who sat on a bank measuring out a fishing line,
watching me come on.

He made room for me beside him
and I wanted to tell him everything—
how the land where I came from was empty,
how it took up all my words,
the trouble I had getting them back.

But how could I tell him about ugly things out there?
How could I bring the rapacious emptiness of video games
and shopping malls into it, their dark corners and winding
        confusions?
How could I explain that the distracted ministrations of grown-ups,
angry and distant, erased everything inside
leaving only the outside for people to fix upon?

I could not explain, I could not say!

After a while I saw I didn't need to,
I saw that his plain face with its clear blue eyes
contained all of the valley's peace and quietness,
and that he wanted nothing more of me
than to sit beside him at the pond's edge and fish.

So I did. We made a pole of twig and string
and he baited it with worm and we fished together in the soft
    downing sun.
I could have stayed forever,
I knew I need never go back,
so perfect was this world,
cupped in evening light,
calm and sweet under a rosette sky.

I had to return, though, to unstop
the word-jam that froze me up,
to locate the words that would tell this story and others.
I didn't know then that learning to talk
would take my whole life;
I only knew I had to try.

I wanted to give him
something to remember me by,
so I gave him an old Petoskey stone from my pocket,
its pocked, time-locked cells smoothed over
by centuries of worrying hands.

He turned it over in his palm
and looked at me with eyes so clear
I could see all the lakes inside him,
how clean they were,
how long they would last.

He put a dash of that cleanness in my hand,
though it took a lifetime to re-find,
and I walked back to the white horizon
where the canvas started and gave way to home.

Witness: Three Poems

> Witness: One who sees.
>> Artist: One who shapes.
> Ghosts: My brother.
>> My brother, and me.
> Witness: One who sees with the mind's eye.

A Boy, A Bike

I.

A boy, a bike, a country lane.

A slender boy,
on a blue bike,
in a cold rain.

Pedaling hard
as though his life depended on it,
as perhaps it did:

In a gray basement,
with a bare bulb and a string hanging down,
stood a man—his father—with a rope.

"I could strangle you with this,"
the man said.

A thick rope,
a golden braid.

II.

Sometime later the boy stole a car,
then another, and still yet one more.

He joined the wires under the dash;
the engine roared and the boy sped off.

He enjoyed the relief he felt driving away;
an expansion in the chest and a feeling of hope—

He could start over anytime, anywhere,
in the town he just passed through or

the one just ahead: a new man, freshly made,
without history or even a name.

III.

The prison walls were deeply gray,
darkly so,
and the bare bulb pressed down from the ceiling
like a big-fingered hand on the back of his neck.

Day and night the doors clanged shut, open
and shut. And every time the men formed a line
for the shower or the yard, someone grabbed his dick
and said "Hey, there, baby, what's this?"

IV.

So he ran again or tried to,
one snowy winter's day—

A hand on the fence;
a foot;
another hand over,

A shout—
from behind him somewhere,
or below—

Still he kept on going:
another foot up,
a hand near the top;

then suddenly a crack—
a single black shot in the back.

V.

And still the snow fell—
white from a grey sky,
red beneath the boy.

The Funeral

A rather inauspicious day for a funeral:
the sky blue, the sun bold,
the leaves budding with green—
an insult almost.

But the ground kept up its part—
the fresh black loam, moist and cool,
crumbled down the sides of the hole
while the priest murmured blessings and chants
until our father, who'd been standing quietly at the grave,
heaved a lung-ripping sob and jumped inside.

He pounded the coffin and called his son's name,
bawling his eyes out and shouting,
"Bobby! Get out of there!
Come on, Bob, goddamn it, get out!"
Fumbling with the latches and muttering,
"Alright, then, I'm coming in after ya, ya little b—"

Suddenly he stopped on the word
and a sob came out instead
and he slumped to his knees,
crying, "My boy,
my boy…."

My uncles knelt in their good suits to haul him out
while the aunts and his mother closed in,
patting his shoulders and murmuring "there, there
there, there."

Meanwhile, my sisters looked on,
wondering about our father's display,
wondering: had the blows been kisses then
and the beatings, love?

Did the sobbing and the fumbling mean
that he'd take it all back if he could?
Replace the dark hole of hatred
with something brighter,
if he could?

History

I want to reach back into history
with the hand of a god
and bring you back.

Sit you next to me in this chair
and hear your story, the whole thing:
what did you laugh about
and who did you love?

Did you like Elvis the best, or the Beatles?
Did you think Steve McQueen was the coolest,
Or James Dean? Paul Newman's hustler
would have been my model—what about yours?

And about those other, much more private things—tell me:
when dad wrapped his hands round your neck and squeezed,
how frightened did you feel? How helpless?

And when he rattled the furnace ducts under the house,
just to let you know he was there—just to let you know
there was no place you could be where he wasn't—
did your brain stutter and your heart skip a beat?

Why did you keep going after the guard said stop?
Because anyplace was better than the places you had been?

Your fraternal twin,
born 20 years too late to conspire or commiserate with,
too late to save your life or soften it,
did you know your death may well have saved mine?

I want to reach back into history
and bring you back,
sit you down beside me in this chair
and you can talk, or we will, or we won't,
though I'm sure after a while we'd snicker
and fall out laughing at something,
but either way, you'd know I was here, I heard you.

Simmering Beneath the Sun

Some days, this sea's a balm:
placid, sun-dappled, a palliative
for wave-watchers and passers-by.

Visitors search for the storied surf in vain—
the sea's too calm, the waves too small.
The sun beams over the ocean like a benevolent grandmother,
illuminating the sea-world in a graceful, lemony light
that streams down evenly the whole day long.

Yet the tides can come in
with the noise of a tornado bearing down on a house
and the undertow of a wave can rake
a body beneath it and never spit it back.

Sometimes a storm builds miles out
and wind lends the water muscle enough
to wrest a new face from the cliffs,
to carve a new coast for the shore.

Next day, the sea's back a balm,
barely a swell to speak of,
the waves a quiet pulse
simmering beneath the sun.

The Flesh of Gods and Roses

Soft at the tear,
like suede worn smooth
by troubled hands;

supple to the frail edge
and fragrant even as the berry-dark
petals begin to fade.

Flesh like ether,
momentary, fickle;
how can the gods be anything but after us—
our image—when this is all we know:

Want and fear of death,
their limits strung by our beads;
our beads knit by habit and desire.

Everything that lives passes away
yet the gods remain,
dressed in the robes we made for them.

Close as a Twin

Close as a twin, sly as a shadow,
My Mortality is following me:

Lock-step beside me every time
I round a corner or
bend to tie a shoe;

bound to me like a corset
and twined to my heartbeat
like an inner tidal dial,

My Mortality hums a constant whisper
in my ear about the dark, about
a blank there's no way out of.

When I finally stop to confront him,
My Mortality shrugs:

"It's not personal," he says,
          enfolding me in fog,
leaving behind my bones.

The Pontoon

The Pontoon is a lazy boat,
big and wide and made for floating.
You can look with curiosity at the shore,
but you can't investigate close up
because the body's too broad.

So you're forced to watch shoreline goings-on from afar,
which can suit one nicely at times—
a-sprawl in a deck chair
or sitting on the pointed front-end of a 'toon,
dangling your legs in the water.

Or you might anchor the boat over the black depths
and dive, cleaving the water with your body,
its perfect pressure holding you up,
holding you in.

You'll probably stay in the water a long time,
you and your cousins or just you.
You'll pretend you're a fish;
your feet are flippers of the most powerful sort;
it's marvelous how they become fins.

You'll swim as long as you can underwater,
your eyes open to the dark,
your entire body a fin.

Then you'll surface and float on your back
or maybe you'll swim overhand to shore
and sit on someone's dock awhile before you return.

When you reach the Pontoon, you'll haul yourself up
and lay a towel on the boat's fat deck
and collapse onto your back
and there you will lie,
breathing hard, each breath
a pleasure because you earned it so well.

After awhile you'll become aware
of birds chirping somewhere, and a dog barking in the distance
(your dog maybe)
and you'll sit up, dazed and at peace.

Sometime later, your mother calls your name
and her voice echoes around the valley,
over the trees and across the water to the boat.

So you crank up the engine
and head for home,
and the next day you do it again,
and after that, again.

Dinner at the Golden Gate

One late sorrow-filled afternoon I went to the park
to read and cry and contemplate suicide.

I found a sunny spot in a vivid, well-watered meadow,
hauled out some books and magazines,
and flipped off my shoes.

I felt quite the misanthrope that afternoon:
I hated the cries of children and darted bitter arrows of annoyance
in their direction whenever they crossed my path.

I despised myself, and found something to dislike in everything I saw:
the leaves too green, the scent of the eucalyptus trees
and the bay leaves too keen; the flowers hideously bright.

All of this and more led me to consider a variety of dark endings for
    myself,
all of which included the further mutilation of an already broken heart,
itself being the source of this fat lot of misery in the first place.

After planning a pleasing dispersal of personal effects,
I turned to reading some Yiyun Li stories in the New Yorker,
stories so despicably beautiful they depressed me even more
and I mewed and bawled through a small packet of tissues.

A reddish-brown blur passing in the distance
interrupted my languor and I looked up to see
a slim red fox with a bushy, black-ringed tail
trotting along the edge of the meadow.

His tail was bigger than his torso,
and he seemed edgy and not entirely sure of himself,
spritely but wary, on the alert it seemed
for something interesting just round the next shrub.

I watched him 'til he was out of sight, completely perked by his
    presence,
wondering what the heck a slim little fox was doing
wandering the busy Botanical Gardens on a Sunday afternoon.

A moment later a giant blue Cardinal flew in,
came to a confident full stop about three feet from my pile of tissues
and looked me straight in the eye.

Not the contemplative type, he lost interest immediately,
pecked the ground a few times and hopped into a bush nearby.

I was attracted by his blueness, which was indeed rather Royal,
and by his bigness—cardinals aren't usually the size of crows, are
    they?—
when a fat brown squirrel leaped into view
carrying a walnut the size of his head in his mouth.

So much for depression and doom, darkness and gloom—
it was dinnertime in the Golden Gate Park!

How very clever of Nature to provide such sly reminders
of how beautifully life would continue
should I be fool enough to leave its carnival before my time.

Far better instead to get some take out
and eat it in the park.

Not Shaped Like a Fist

The heart is not an organ,
nor it is a muscle
and it is not shaped like a fist.

Instead, it is shaped like a coil—an intestine—
and when someone you love dies,
your chest is ripped open at the lung,
and your heart coil is gripped like a sausage by a butcher,
who yanks it out section by section,
and squeezes and shakes each one with glee.

When he's done, he stuffs the bloody coil back in,
hastily sometimes, it's all the same to him.

The blood is a little frightening but
you patch yourself up as best you can
and try to get them back—
try to grip your mother's arm and pull her over
or grab your brother's hand and bring him home.

That's when you learn the dead are irretrievable:
locked firmly behind death's iron door,
on which our fists leave no mark
and our breath, not even a film.

Metal Washing Metal with Fire

They arrived on several ships
from all seven continents—
cats and dogs carrying guns:

assault rifles, pistols, revolvers;
semi-automatics, machine guns,
shotguns, carbines, and service rifles,

all belonging (formerly)
to their humans who
seem to have lost their way,

leaving right action
and clear seeing to
the animals who loved them.

At the top of Mt. Etna,
Hephaestus and his men heaved
the guns by the half-ton
into the mountain's smoking mouth,

pushing the barrels, clips,
shafts and shanks down
the volcano's fiery throat

into the earth's liquid core,
metal washing metal with fire,
making it useful again,

part of the earth that sustains
us, rather than the fear
and hate that divide us.

Man Standing on the Backbone of the Sea

The scalloped brown reef—
    revealed at low tide—
gleamed in the sunlight,
    its dark teeth grinning,
its back curving out to sea.

Standing on a sliver of spine
    the fisherman held his line high
as a big Chinook took the bait
    and dove with it under the waves.
He braced his boots against the rocks

    and pulled back on the line. Overhead
the sun carved out the path of its setting
    as the puny man, a mere shadow
in the sun's eye, set his will against
    the salmon's and reeled him in.

Death in Ericè

The fog howled in off the sea
and kept its hungry fingers close to the ground,
eating up dogs.

The public square was empty of chairs
and the villagers stayed indoors
standing at curtained windows, lifting
languid hands to close the folds.

Thin-skinned dogs crept through the streets at night,
their nails clacking on stones as they poked in alleys,
sniffing out bones.

One night I listened as one of the males
stalked a rabbit outside the village wall.
At first the rabbit mewed as it ran,
emitting sharp little hiccups of fright.

But when the dog caught it,
amid the crackle of twigs
and the breakage of bramble,
the rabbit's quiet lit the dark.

Judith Beheading Holofernes

In Caravaggio's rendering,
Judith holds the head at some remove:

      from the task,
which is gruesome and difficult—
the neck thick with muscles, bones—
      and from herself, from
the deed she is doing.

When she is finished,
she wraps the head in a cloth
and steals through narrow alleys
'til reaching the temple doors.

There she presents the fruit
of her labor to the elders in Bethulia—
a strong girl with a quiet face,
her smock still bloody,
Nolofernes' wrecked head in her hands.

The elders alert the Hebrew army
to the enemy leader's demise
and consider their surprise—

the course of war changed not
by the wit and might of their own soldiers, but
by the guts and wiles of a strange young woman,
dangerous and bold.

Hunter

Stealth is in the way he climbs the tree:
slowly, his hands and feet bearing
the weight of his body, his fingers
gripping the bark, wrapping
around the limbs, pulling.

Braced, he's the landscape:
pale inside winter's bright chill,
cool under the faint hum of a waking sun,
quiet, like the snow falling,
waiting.

His bow is the tender brown of frozen earth,
a branch among branches. Its string pulled tight,
like the muscles in his arms as he poises the arrow,
the roses of his breath floating like birds on the morning air.

The arrow when it flies cuts the air with a hush
and meets the deer's chest with a thud.
Her long legs buckle one joint at a time,
her life soon closed in the early morning light,
his renewed by the artfulness of the chase,
its triumphant end.

About the Author

"We shall not cease from exploration / and the end of all our exploring
will be to arrive where we started / and know the place for the first time."
—T.S. Eliot, *Little Gidding*

In 2024, **Ms. Gibson** surprised herself by moving back to Michigan
after 27 years in other parts of the country—two years in Connecticut;
eight years in the San Francisco Bay Area; fifteen years in Atlanta; a
year or two in Minnesota. In 2020, she started feeling homesick for
the marshes and lakes of mid- and western Michigan where she grew
up and went to college. Ms. Gibson missed the area's spaciousness—
farmland that stretches for miles between roads; Lake Michigan; sand
dunes; snow; and a spring season that take months to unfurl rather
than weeks. She also missed the slower pace of life. So she bought a
house—her first!—in Lansing, the state's capitol, a small, (mostly)
progressive working-class town built near the banks of the Grand
and the Red Cedar rivers. Michigan State University, from which
she received a B.A. in English and Creative Writing and an M.A. in
American studies, is next door, in East Lansing, and lends the area the
resources of a friendly, active college town.

To earn a living, Ms. Gibson has worked as a technical writer for nearly
30 years, mostly part-time until 2019, when she joined the Georgia
Tech Research Institute (GTRI) in Atlanta as a full-time researcher
and writer. She is not technically inclined but can explain sometimes
complicated things clearly for non-technical audiences (since she is
one herself). She is grateful for the smart, collegial colleagues at GTRI
who kindly supported her out of state move in 2024.

Ms. Gibson feels lucky to have lived in so many different parts of the
country for as long as she did; she thinks she is better in every way for
the experiences she's had in each, for the people she's met, the friends
she's made, and for the failures and successes she's experienced.

On the mundane plane of daily, non-working life, Ms. Gibson enjoys
reading, drawing, cooking, swimming, meditating, writing, animals
(especially cats) and being outside doing just about anything (including
shoveling snow and mowing the lawn!), grateful for life's beauty and
heft, for the wonder and strangeness of it all.

www.ingramcontent.com/pod-product-compliance
Lightning Source LLC
Chambersburg PA
CBHW020222090426
42734CB00008B/1185